# BOOM SCIENCE

# SEASONS

**Georgia Amson-Bradshaw**

WAYLAND
www.waylandbooks.co.uk

Published in paperback in Great Britain in 2019 by Wayland

Copyright © Hodder and Stoughton Limited, 2018

Produced for Wayland by
White-Thomson Publishing Ltd
www.wtpub.co.uk

Series Editor: Georgia Amson-Bradshaw
Series Designer: Rocket Design (East Anglia) Ltd

ISBN: 978 1 5263 0649 4
10 9 8 7 6 5 4 3 2 1

MIX
Paper from
responsible sources
FSC® C104740

Wayland
An imprint of
Hachette Children's Group
Part of Hodder & Stoughton
Carmelite House
50 Victoria Embankment
London EC4Y 0DZ

An Hachette UK Company
www.hachette.co.uk
www.hachettechildrens.co.uk

Printed in China

Picture acknowledgements:

Images from Shutterstock.com: Hannamariah 6c, Anastasia Mazeina 7bl, AlenaLitvin 9t, Vladimir Sazonov 12br, NotionPic 13t, SavAleKon14b, John Gomez 15t, topseller 15b, Doremi 16, Jaroslav Moravcik 17t, Ignat Zaytsev 17bl, Olha Solodenko 17br, dzenphoto 20t, zaxenart 20b, photomaster 21t, GraphicsRF 24t, LiuSol 25b, violetblue 26t, Piotr Wawrzyniuk 26b, Alena Kaz 27b. Images from wiki commons: Daniel Ramirez 6b, Zoë Helene Kindermann 21b

All illustrations on pages 12, 13, 18, 19, 22, 23 by Steve Evans

All design elements from Shutterstock.

Glossary words are shown in bold.

# CONTENTS

# CHANGING SEASONS

Spring, summer, autumn and winter are all seasons.

## FOUR SEASONS

Lots of countries around the world have four seasons. Each season brings different weather, and the length of the day changes.

spring

summer

autumn

winter

## WET AND DRY

Some countries, near the middle of the Earth, stay warm all year round. They have just two seasons: a rainy season and a dry season.

rainy

dry

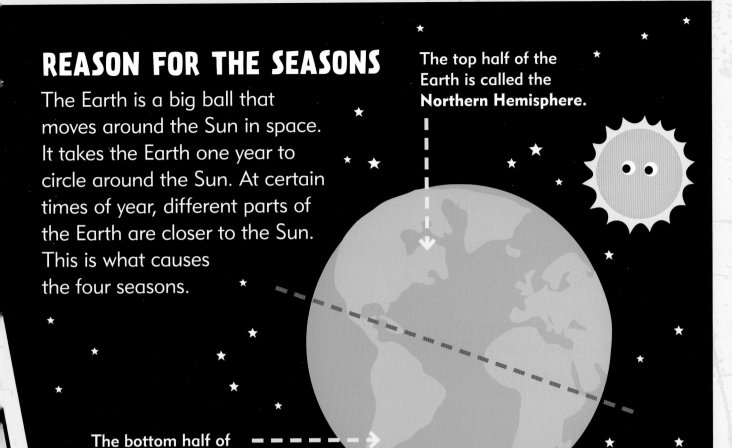

# REASON FOR THE SEASONS

The Earth is a big ball that moves around the Sun in space. It takes the Earth one year to circle around the Sun. At certain times of year, different parts of the Earth are closer to the Sun. This is what causes the four seasons.

The top half of the Earth is called the **Northern Hemisphere.**

The bottom half of the Earth is called the **Southern Hemisphere.**

# SUMMER HERE, WINTER THERE

The seasons don't happen at the same time all over the world. When it is summer in the Northern Hemisphere, it is winter in the Southern Hemisphere. When it is winter in the Northern Hemisphere, it is summer in the Southern Hemisphere.

# SPRING

In spring, the days get longer and the weather gets warmer.

## SPRING TO LIFE

After the cold, dark winter, nature starts to come to life again in the spring. The temperature begins to rise and there is more daylight.

## LONGER DAYS

During spring, the days get longer and the nights get shorter. For one day in spring, night and day are exactly the same length. We call this the **equinox**. It happens in March in the Northern Hemisphere, and September in the Southern Hemisphere.

12 HOURS

## APRIL SHOWERS

The weather in spring can change a lot. Some days are warm and sunny, but the weather can quickly become cold and windy. Spring often brings rain showers.

# WOW!

Spring gets its name from 'springing time', which was the old name for the season. It is the time when new plants 'spring' from the earth.

### HIDE and SEEK

When the weather is rainy and sunny at the same time, it can create a very special effect. Do you know what it is? Can you spot one hiding? Answer on page 28.

# MAKE A RAIN GAUGE

Measure how much rain falls each day in spring with a homemade rain gauge. You'll need:

A permanent marker pen

Some scissors

A two-litre plastic bottle

A ruler

## STEP ONE

Cut off the tapered top part of the bottle. This can be tricky, so ask an adult to do this part. Place the cut-off part upside down, inside the main body of the bottle.

## STEP TWO

Using the ruler and the permanent marker pen, mark a scale up the side of the bottle in centimetres, starting at the bottom.

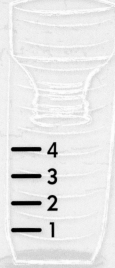

## STEP THREE

Take your rain gauge outside. Ensure it won't blow over by burying the bottom part a few centimetres into the ground.

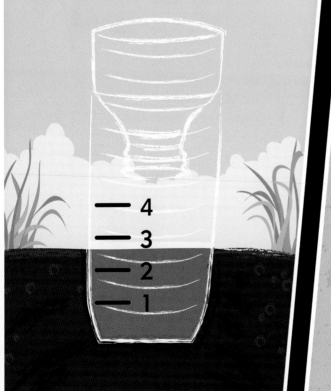

## STEP FOUR

After it has rained, check to see how far up the scale the water has risen. Empty out the water and replace your rain gauge, ready to begin recording again. Keep a record of how many centimetres of rain fall each day.

| Date | Rainfall |
| --- | --- |
| 7 May | 0.5 cm |
| 8 May | 2 cm |
| 9 May | 0 cm |

# SUMMER

Summer is the warmest season of the year.

## HOTTING UP

In summer, everything is bursting with life. Bees buzz about, birds chirp and chatter in the trees, and flowers bloom in the hot sun. June, July and August are the summer months in the Northern Hemisphere.

In the Southern Hemisphere, summer is in December, January and February.

What do you call a snowman in July?

A puddle! Ha ha!

## HEY, WHAT AM I?

This fuzzy insect is very busy in summer. What is it?
Answer on page 28.

# SUMMER SUN

The weather in summer is often hot and sunny. Some days have a gentle **breeze**, but other days are very still and **humid**. As well as hot sunshine, summer can bring dramatic storms with thunder and lightning.

## MIDSUMMER

Long summer days are perfect for picnics! The longest day of the year is called the **summer solstice**, or midsummer.

## STAYING SAFE

It feels great to play outside in the sunshine, but it's important to stay safe. Always wear sun cream to stop your skin from burning. Drink lots of water to stay **hydrated**.

# AUTUMN

In autumn, the days get shorter and the weather gets colder.

## WINDING DOWN

Autumn is another season of change. The temperature gets cooler, and the Sun sets a little earlier each day. The leaves on **deciduous trees** change colour and fall to the ground.

# WOW!

Until the 1500s, autumn was called 'harvest', because it is the time of year when people would harvest their crops.

# MISTS AND FROSTS

Some autumn days are very clear and sunny. After a clear night in late autumn, the ground might be covered by sparkling frost. Other autumn days can be grey, wet and windy. Sometimes in the mornings and evenings, there is fog or mist in the air.

Frosty leaves are caused by ice crystals forming when the temperature falls below freezing point.

## HEY, WHAT AM I?

You often see this vegetable in autumn. What is it? Answer on page 28.

## HIDE AND SEEK

There is an equinox in autumn, as well as in spring. Can you spot a sun and a moon hiding? Answer on page 28.

# WINTER

Winter is the coldest season of the year.

## COLD AND DARK

In winter, there are fewer animals to be seen, and deciduous trees are bare of leaves. The nights are long and the temperature is colder. December, January and February are the winter months in the Northern Hemisphere. In the Southern Hemisphere, winter is in June, July and August.

## HIDE AND SEEK

Can you spot four snowflakes hiding? Answer on page 28.

## LET IT SNOW

Winter weather is cold, even when the Sun is shining. On very cold winter days, water droplets in the air become ice and fall to the ground as snow.

When is sunrise?

In about three months!

Changes in the number of daylight hours are more extreme close to the Earth's poles. During winter at the **North Pole**, the Sun doesn't rise at all for 11 weeks!

### HEY, WHAT AM I?

Dripping water can freeze when the temperature drops below zero degrees Celsius. What can you see in this picture?
Answer on page 29.

# YOUR TURN!

# MAKE FROST

See how frost forms on cold surfaces with this super cool experiment. You'll need:

**An empty tin can**

**Some crushed ice (see step one)**

**Some water**

**Table salt**

## STEP ONE

Ask an adult to help you make crushed ice, by wrapping ice cubes in a cloth or bag and crushing them with something heavy, such as a rolling pin. Half-fill the tin can with crushed ice. Add four tablespoons of table salt and a splash of water. Mix well.

**Be careful of sharp tin edges!**

Let the tin sit for a few minutes. Watch it while you wait, and you will see frost forming on the part of the tin where the ice and salt mixture is cooling the metal.

## STEP THREE

Think about the frost on your can, and the frost that forms outside in autumn and winter. Where do you think it comes from? Why do you think it forms? Answer on page 29.

# ANIMALS

## Animal behaviour changes with the seasons.

## NEW LIFE

Spring is the season when most animals have babies. Birds build nests and raise chicks. Insects such as bumblebees wake up out of a very deep sleep, called **hibernation**. They begin to **reproduce** in spring.

## THE HIGH LIFE

In summer, there is a lot of food around. **Migratory** animals and birds that spent the winter elsewhere arrive in summer to enjoy the warm weather and tasty plants and insects.

Mosquitoes... yum yum!

## STOCKING UP

Autumn is a time to prepare for the winter. Animals such as squirrels collect nuts and store them to get them through the winter ahead. Migratory birds and animals leave to go back to warmer countries.

## HIDE AND SEEK

Can you spot five nuts that a squirrel has hidden? Answer on page 29.

## WINTER SLEEP

The weather is cold, and there is less food in winter. Some animals, such as dormice, go into hibernation. They spend the whole winter asleep in their cosy nests.

# YOUR TURN!

# BUILD A BUG HOTEL

Provide insects with a place to hibernate with this crafty science activity. You'll need:

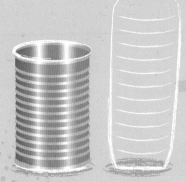

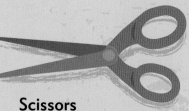
Scissors

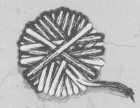
A ball of string

Some empty tin cans OR empty plastic bottles

Lots of natural materials such as twigs, pinecones, lengths of bamboo, stones and bark

## STEP ONE

If you are using plastic bottles for your bug hotel, cut the tops off.

Ask an adult to help you with the cutting!

## STEP TWO

Fill your tins or cut-down plastic bottles with your natural materials. Pack them in tightly, creating small nooks and crannies for bugs to squeeze in between.

Be careful of sharp tin edges!

## STEP THREE

Using the string, tie your filled tins or bottles together. You can then either hang your finished bug hotel from a tree, or place it on the ground. Depending on where you put it, you will attract different insect guests.

# PLANTS
## Plant growth follows the seasons.

## GREEN SHOOTS

Plants need warmth and sunlight to grow. After the cold, dark winter, plants put out new shoots in the spring. Deciduous trees grow new leaves and flower buds.

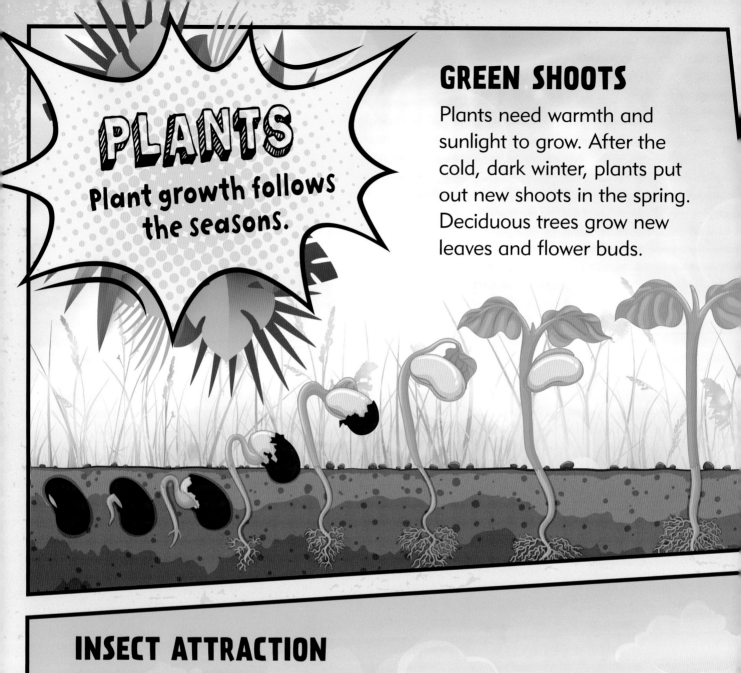

## INSECT ATTRACTION

The long days of summer give plants the sunlight they need to grow. Flowers bloom, attracting busy insects. Travelling insects **pollinate** the flowers, helping the plants to reproduce.

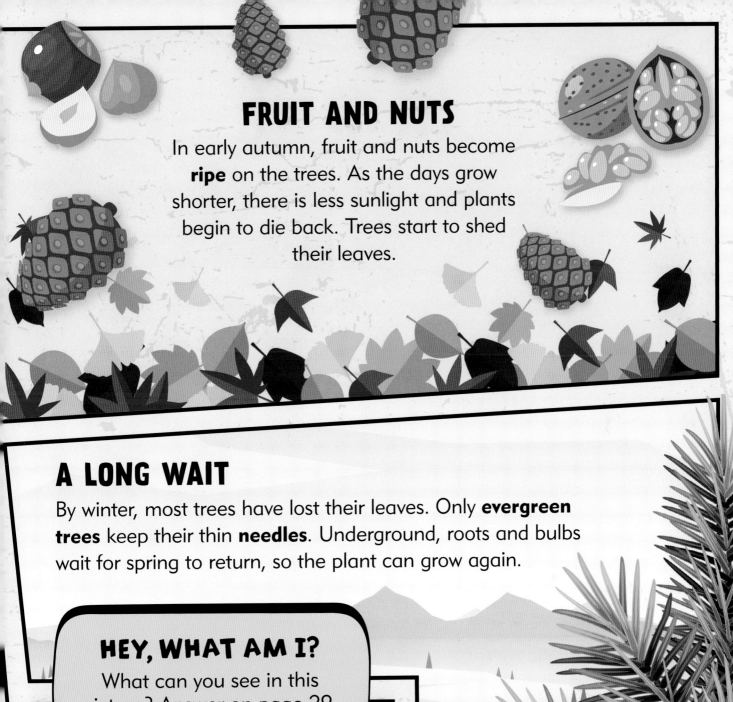

# FRUIT AND NUTS

In early autumn, fruit and nuts become **ripe** on the trees. As the days grow shorter, there is less sunlight and plants begin to die back. Trees start to shed their leaves.

## A LONG WAIT

By winter, most trees have lost their leaves. Only **evergreen trees** keep their thin **needles**. Underground, roots and bulbs wait for spring to return, so the plant can grow again.

### HEY, WHAT AM I?

What can you see in this picture? Answer on page 29.

# CELEBRATIONS

Around the world, people celebrate the seasons in different ways.

## SPRING RETURNS

Many **cultures** around the world celebrate the arrival of spring. In Japan, cherry blossom parties are held to celebrate the arrival of the pretty spring flowers.

## FUN IN SUMMER

In Sweden, the longest day of the year is celebrated with a midsummer **festival**. People dance around **maypoles** and wear crowns made of flowers.

# HALLOWEEN

In the past, **Celtic people** celebrated **Samhain**. It was the end of the harvest, and the start of the darker half of the year. It was believed to be a night when ghosts returned to the land of the living! This **tradition** has changed over time to become Halloween in some countries.

## WINTER CHEER

Having a feast and a celebration in the middle of winter is a tradition found in many countries. In the Northern Hemisphere, Christmas is a holiday that is celebrated close to midwinter. However, in the Southern Hemisphere, Christmas falls in the middle of summer!

Ho Ho Ho, dudes!

# ANSWERS

Page 9

**Hide and Seek** A rainbow

Page 12

**What am I?** I'm a bumblebee.

Page 15

**What am I?** I'm a pumpkin

Page 15

**Hide and Seek** Sun and moon

Page 16

**Hide and Seek** Snowflakes

**Page 17**

**What am I?** I'm icicles on a building.

**Page 21** **Hide and Seek** Nuts

**ANIMALS**
Animal behaviour changes with the seasons.

**NEW LIFE**
Spring is the season when animals have babies. Birds build nests and raise chicks. Insects such as bumblebees wake up out of a very deep sleep, called **hibernation**. They begin to **reproduce** in spring.

**THE HIGH LIFE**
In summer there is a lot of food around. **Migratory** animals and birds that spent the winter elsewhere arrive in summer to enjoy the warm weather, and tasty grass and insects.

Mosquitos... yum yum!

**STOCKING UP**
Autumn is a time to prepare for the winter. Animals such as squirrels collect nuts and store them to get them through the winter ahead. Migratory birds and animals leave to go back to warmer countries.

**HIDE and SEEK**
Can you spot five nuts that a squirrel has hidden? Answer on page 29.

**WINTER SLEEP**
The weather is cold, and there is less food in winter. Some animals, such as dormice, hibernation. They spend the winter asleep in their cosy homes.

20

21

**Page 25**

**What am I?** I'm new leaves growing on a tree branch in spring.

**Page 19**

**Your turn** Frost

Frost forms on the side of the can because there is always some water in the air. We just can't see it. When the water in the air touches the very cold can, the water droplets freeze and turn into frost on the side of the can. A similar thing happens with frost outside. Grass and leaves get very cold in the cold weather. When water in the air touches the leaves, it forms frost.

# GLOSSARY

**breeze** a gentle wind

**Celtic people** a group of people who lived in ancient Britain, Ireland and parts of France

**culture** a group of people with particular beliefs and ways of living

**deciduous trees** trees that lose their leaves during winter

**equinox** a date in the year when the day and the night last the same number of hours

**evergreen trees** trees that do not lose their leaves in winter

**festival** a time or event of celebration

**hibernation** when animals go into a deep sleep during the cold winter season

**humid** when the air is holding a lot of water

**hydrated** to have had enough water to drink

**maypole** a tall pole decorated with flowers and ribbons for dancing around

**migratory** animals that travel long distances each year to find food or places to raise young

**needles** the thin pointy leaves that some types of tree have, such as pine trees

**North Pole** the most northern point on the Earth

**Northern Hemisphere** the part of the Earth that is north of the equator

**pollinate** when insects carry pollen from one flower to another, which helps the flowers reproduce

**reproduce** to have offspring or young

**ripe** fruit that is fully grown and ready to be eaten

**Samhain** a Celtic celebration that marked the end of harvest and the beginning of winter

**Southern Hemisphere** the part of the Earth that is south of the equator

**summer solstice** the date during the year when the night is shortest and the day is longest

**tradition** a belief or an activity that started in the past and has been carried on

# INDEX

# Boom Science Series contents lists

## ELECTRICITY

- ★ ELECTRICITY AND ENERGY
- ★ USING ELECTRICITY
- ★ YOUR TURN: Electricity hunt
- ★ NATURAL ELECTRICITY
- ★ BATTERIES
- ★ CIRCUITS
- ★ YOUR TURN: Make a battery
- ★ SWITCHES
- ★ MAKING ELECTRICITY
- ★ STAYING SAFE
- ★ YOUR TURN: Make a switch

## FORCES

- ★ PUSHES AND PULLS
- ★ GRAVITY
- ★ WEIGHT
- ★ YOUR TURN: Forces at the playground
- ★ FRICTION
- ★ WATER RESISTANCE
- ★ AIR RESISTANCE
- ★ YOUR TURN: Make a parachute
- ★ MAGNETS
- ★ SIMPLE MACHINES
- ★ YOUR TURN: Make simple machines

## HUMAN BODY

- ★ HEALTHY BODY
- ★ SKELETON AND BONES
- ★ MUSCLES
- ★ YOUR TURN: Make a model arm
- ★ DIGESTIVE SYSTEM
- ★ HEART AND BLOOD
- ★ BREATHING
- ★ YOUR TURN: How big are your lungs?
- ★ BRAIN AND NERVES
- ★ SENSES
- ★ YOUR TURN: Test your senses

## LIGHT

- ★ BRIGHT LIGHT
- ★ SOURCES OF LIGHT
- ★ SEEING
- ★ YOUR TURN: Eyes vs. brain trick
- ★ BOUNCING LIGHT
- ★ LIGHT AND MATERIALS
- ★ SHADOWS
- ★ YOUR TURN: Silhouette portraits
- ★ LIVING THINGS
- ★ USING LIGHT
- ★ YOUR TURN: Chat using light

## MATERIALS

- ★ MATERIALS
- ★ USING MATERIALS
- ★ PROPERTIES
- ★ YOUR TURN: Waterproof materials
- ★ NATURAL MATERIALS
- ★ MAN-MADE MATERIALS
- ★ YOUR TURN: Sorting materials
- ★ SOLIDS
- ★ LIQUIDS AND GASES
- ★ HEATING AND COOLING MATERIALS
- ★ YOUR TURN: Freezing materials

## PLANTS

- ★ PLANTS
- ★ ROOTS AND STEMS
- ★ YOUR TURN: Colour change celery
- ★ LEAVES
- ★ FLOWERS
- ★ FRUIT
- ★ SEEDS AND BULBS
- ★ YOUR TURN: Grow a bulb in water
- ★ SUNLIGHT
- ★ WATER AND WARMTH
- ★ YOUR TURN: Plant maze

## SEASONS

- ★ CHANGING SEASONS
- ★ SPRING
- ★ YOUR TURN: Make a rain gauge
- ★ SUMMER
- ★ AUTUMN
- ★ WINTER
- ★ YOUR TURN: Make frost
- ★ ANIMALS
- ★ YOUR TURN: Build a bug hotel
- ★ PLANTS
- ★ CELEBRATIONS

## SOUND

- ★ SOUND ALL AROUND
- ★ MOVING SOUND
- ★ HEARING
- ★ YOUR TURN: Improve your ears
- ★ LOUD AND QUIET SOUNDS
- ★ HIGH AND LOW SOUNDS
- ★ MUSIC
- ★ YOUR TURN: Form a band
- ★ ECHOES
- ★ SOUND AND MATERIALS
- ★ YOUR TURN: Hear secret sounds